Published by Creative Education
123 South Broad Street, Mankato, Minnesota 56001
Creative Education is an imprint of The Creative Company

Art direction by Rita Marshall
Production design by The Design Lab

Photographs by AP/ Wide World (Eric Risberg), Artemis Images (ATD Group, Inc.,
Indianapolis Motor Speedway, Tim O'Hara, Pikes Peak International Hill Climb),
Cleo Photography, Corbis (Giry Daniel, Duomo/William Sallaz, Tim Wright), Creatas,
Defense Visual Information Center, Herbert L. Gatewood, Getty Images (Michael Malyszko),
Anne Gordon, Sally McCrae Kuyper, Alan Look, Doug Mitchel, National Air and Space
Museum (Smithsonian Institute), Bonnie Sue Rauch, D. Jeanene Tiner, Toyota

Library of Congress Cataloging-in-Publication Data

Tiner, John Hudson, 1944–
Cars / by John Hudson Tiner.
p. cm. — (Let's investigate)
Summary: An introduction to the history of automobiles and to various vehicles
of the past, present, and future.
ISBN 1-58341-256-5
1. Automobiles—Juvenile literature. [1. Automobiles.] I. Title. II. Series.
TL147 .T55   2003
629.222—dc21   2002031487

First edition

2 4 6 8 9 7 5 3 1

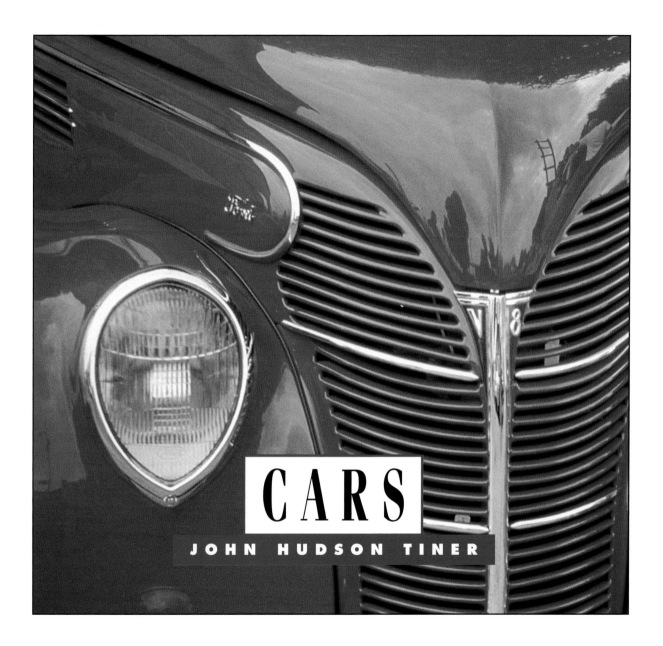

CARS

JOHN HUDSON TINER

Creative 🍎 Education

C A R
CRAWL

The world's first car, built by Frenchman Joseph Cugnot, could go no faster than a slow walk—about 2.3 miles (3.7 km) per hour.

C A R
CARRIAGE

The first cars were known as horseless carriages because they were hardly more than a horse-drawn carriage powered by a small gasoline engine.

Cars are the world's most widely used form of transportation

4

The first cars were sold to the public in the 1890s, but only a few people could afford them. Cars cost a lot of money. They also needed skilled mechanics to repair them, and trained drivers to operate them. The number of cars increased as vehicles became safer, easier to drive, and cheap enough for ordinary people to own. By the year 2000, roadways around the world carried more than 500 million vehicles.

6

Above, the Stanley Steamer
Right, a steam-powered cart

THE FIRST CARS

Until the 1700s, people traveled over land by muscle power—either their own muscles or those of animals such as horses, oxen, or camels. In 1769, Frenchman Joseph Cugnot built the first vehicle, a three-wheeled cart, that ran on its own power. A **steam engine** powered his cart. But his invention proved too heavy and clumsy to turn easily. During his first public test, Cugnot crashed into a wall.

7

The future of the car was with an **internal combustion engine**. Inventors developed a gasoline engine that had a **piston** in a metal cylinder. The piston compressed an explosive mixture of gas and air. An electric spark set off the mixture, and the expanding gases drove the piston down with great force. The piston turned a crank attached to a **drive shaft**, putting a vehicle's wheels in motion.

An internal combustion engine from the 1890s

The Buick was the first car with a windshield. The car was named after its builder, David Dunbar Buick, who invented the windshield.

Early cars were often regarded as symbols of a person's wealth

By 1890, automakers in Germany, France, and the United States were installing gasoline engines in cars. Gottlieb Daimler, a German inventor, built a car that traveled at 10 miles (16 km) per hour. However, the first cars made by him and others were large, expensive, and difficult to keep running.

CARS FOR EVERYONE

Henry Ford, who lived in Detroit, Michigan, worked at a factory that made engines. He believed he could make a car that was inexpensive and reliable. He built his first gasoline engine in 1893, and his first working automobile in 1896. He continued to work after-hours in his own shop. He learned a lot about cars and experimented with ways to improve them. In 1903, he founded the Ford Motor Company to build simple, rugged cars. By 1907, he had a car design he liked. He called it the Model T.

CAR NAME

In 1901, American mechanic Ramson E. Olds built a car that traveled at 18 miles (30 km) per hour. He called it an Oldsmobile, starting a line of cars still built today.

Henry Ford's famous Model T

C A R

Henry Ford named cars by letters of the alphabet. His famous Model T, also known as the Tin Lizzie, came in only one color—black.

The Ford Motor Company produced thousands of cars using assembly lines

Ford built a moving assembly line to make cars quickly and cheaply. As the unfinished car came down the line, each worker had a single task to do, such as screwing on a fender. Overhead conveyor belts delivered parts to the workers. Ford's assembly line lowered the cost of manufacturing, and the price of a car fell from about $950 in 1909 to $290 in 1926. The rugged Model T withstood potholes on city streets and rough country roads. On a good road, it could go a brisk 45 miles (72 km) per hour.

Rolls-Royce is a British automobile company that makes world-famous luxury cars. In 1907, it built a car called the Silver Ghost, so named because of its color and quiet engine.

A t first, operating a car required strength and skill. To start a car, the driver stood in front of it and turned a crank. Sometimes the gas ignited too soon and the engine suddenly ran backwards. When such a "backfire" occurred, the crank flipped backwards with enough force to break a person's arm. In 1911, the makers of a car called the Cadillac added an electric starter. Pressing a button powered an electric motor that cranked the engine.

Above, the Rolls-Royce Silver Ghost
Left, starting a car by crank

C A R
BASICS

The first cars did not have speedometers to measure speed, windshield wipers to clean the windshield, or gas gauges to indicate how much fuel was in the gas tank.

C A R
LAWS

The speed limit for cars in England in the 1800s was four miles (6.4 km) per hour in the country and three miles (4.8 km) per hour in the city.

Night driving became safer with the development of the electric starter and headlight

A battery provided electricity for the car's starter. After the engine started, a **generator** charged the battery. Electric headlights replaced kerosene lanterns for driving at night. By 1920, virtually all new cars were equipped with electric headlights and starters. Some drivers also installed radios so they could listen to music as they traveled.

The first cars had manual **transmissions**, or gearboxes. Gears of different sizes sent power from the engine to the wheels along the drive shaft. First gear produced a lot of power but at a slow speed. As a car accelerated, the driver shifted to gears that produced less power but faster speed. Most cars had a reverse gear and four forward gears.

C   A   R
STATIC

*The first car radios could be played only when the engine was off because, with the engine running, **spark plugs** produced static (electrical noise) that made it difficult to hear.*

13

The shifting of a car's gears results in an increase or decrease in speed

Shifting gears took skill. The driver began by letting up slightly on the gas pedal and pressing down on the **clutch** pedal with the other foot. Then the driver moved the gear lever to the new gear, let up on the clutch, and gave the car gas. When done correctly, passengers hardly noticed the change. When done poorly, the car jolted suddenly, and the gears made a loud grinding noise.

The gear lever of a car with a manual, or "stick shift," transmission

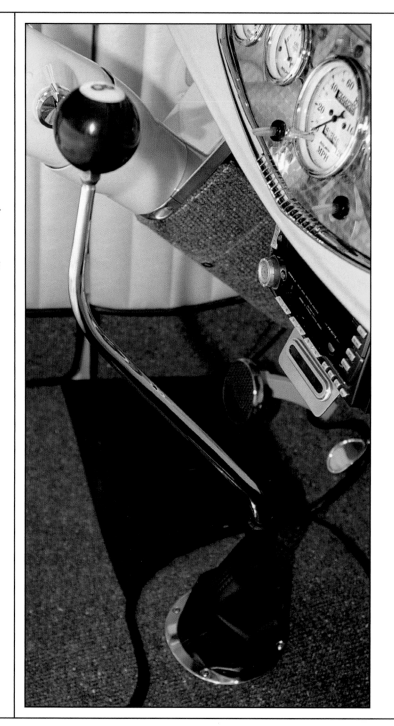

In the 1940s, the Oldsmobile Company installed the first automatic transmissions in its cars. All the driver had to do was press the gas pedal, and the transmission shifted to the correct gear automatically as the speed increased or decreased. Most cars today have automatic transmissions, although some people still prefer cars in which they can shift the gears themselves.

CAR
BUG

Engineer Ferdinand Porsche convinced the German government in 1937 to build a low-priced car called the Volkswagen (German for "people's car"). It later became known as the "Beetle."

Above, a Beetle
Left, an automatic
transmission

CAR
GEARS

Many cars have five forward gears. The fifth one is called overdrive. A car goes into overdrive when it reaches a speed of about 55 miles (89 km) per hour.

16

Brake lights and anti-locking brakes are key safety features

SAFER CARS

Today's cars have many features designed to improve the safety of drivers and passengers. The driver signals left or right turns with orange-colored signal lights. When the driver presses the brake pedal, red brake lights come on, warning drivers in back that the car is slowing down. If a car breaks down along a busy highway, the driver sets front and rear signal lights to flash on and off as a caution to other drivers.

In 1920, half of the cars in the world were Model Ts. Today, about one-third of all cars in the world are found in the U.S.

17

A person of ordinary strength can turn and stop a big car with little effort because power steering and power brakes use small motors to help the driver turn and stop.

A driver can lose control of the car if the wheels start skidding. In the 1980s, anti-locking brakes were developed to prevent skids in a sudden stop. **Sensors** detect when a wheel is no longer rolling and turn off the brake to that wheel for a fraction of a second. The tire regains traction, and the car comes to a controlled stop.

It is critical that tires maintain a firm grip on the road at all times

In the year 2000, the three best-selling cars in the U.S. were the Honda Accord, Toyota Camry, and Ford Taurus. More than 350,000 of each model were sold.

S ometimes collisions cannot be avoided. Cars have bumpers to absorb the shock of low-speed collisions. In a high-speed collision, the steel frame of the car gives way to help absorb the energy of the crash. Although the repairs are more expensive, this crumpling effect reduces injuries.

Above, a Toyota Camry convertible
Left, the crumpling effect of collisions

CAR
FARE

A taxi, or taxicab, is a car whose driver carries passengers for a fare. Usually, the fare is determined by either time or distance.

*Above, taxicabs
Right, child safety
seats help to protect
young passengers*

Seat belts provide additional safety. Small children and babies ride in specially designed safety seats that are firmly secured in the back seat. In a modern car, a bag about three feet (91 cm) across is folded up and tucked into the center of the steering wheel. Another one is located in the dashboard (the panel at the front of the car) on the passenger side. If a sensor detects a serious crash, it releases compressed air. The air bags inflate in about one-tenth of a second, cushioning the driver and passenger. Starting in 1998, all new cars sold in the U.S. had to be equipped with air bags.

O ne of the drawbacks to using cars is the **pollution** they create. The proper mixture of fuel and oxygen in engines reduces the pollutants, and mechanics tune engines so they run properly. Even so, some pollution escapes from the engine and is released into the **exhaust**. The exhaust is run through a device called a **catalytic converter** that changes some of the pollution into gases that are not as harmful.

C A R
CONVERTER

A catalytic converter for reducing pollution from a car's exhaust contains platinum, a metal that is more valuable than gold.

C A R
SPRINT

*In a drag race, two **dragsters** line up beside one another. When the signal light turns green, they thunder one-fourth of a mile (400 m) to a finish line.*

Car exhaust contributes to the smog, or pollution, over many big cities

C A R

In 1979, the U.S. military replaced the jeep with a more powerful, rugged vehicle. Its official name is High Mobility Multi-purpose Wheeled Vehicle, but most people call it a "humvee" for short.

Above, a humvee Right, the jeep was a valuable military vehicle in World War II

OFF-ROAD VEHICLES

During World War II (1939–1945), the U.S. military built a vehicle to travel on highways damaged by bombs and across fields that had no roads. It was called a General Purpose (GP) vehicle. The abbreviation GP was pronounced "jeep." In most vehicles, power is sent to either the two rear wheels (rear-wheel drive) or the two front wheels (front-wheel drive). The jeep's engine sent power to all four of its wheels (all-wheel drive). If two of the wheels got stuck in mud, the other two wheels on dry land could pull the jeep out.

Jeeps proved popular as off-road vehicles, also known as all-**terrain** vehicles (ATVs). ATVs are popular today as sport vehicles. Many drivers enjoy the challenge and freedom of driving ATVs through deserts or over rocky terrain. ATVs with balloon-like tires for driving over sand dunes and along beaches are known as dune buggies.

23

Above, stock cars
Left, ATVs come in a variety of forms

C A R

America's best-known racetrack is the Indianapolis Motor Speedway near Indianapolis, Indiana, where a 500-mile (805 km) race is held each year.

24

C A R
COST

At a cost of $38 million, the Lunar Rover was the most expensive car ever made. It had to be left behind on the moon when the astronauts returned to Earth.

The Lunar Rover was the first wheeled vehicle driven in space

In 1971, the *Lunar Rover* set a record as the passenger vehicle used farther off-road than any other. During the Apollo 15 mission to the moon, astronaut James B. Irwin drove this specially built car over the moon's uneven surface. The *Lunar Rover* was about the size of a golf cart, and electric batteries gave it a top speed of nine miles (14 km) per hour.

In 1997, a new land speed record was set when a race car called the Thrust SSC traveled faster than the speed of sound (which is about 741 miles, or 1,193 km, per hour). The car was powered by two jet engines that together produced about 100,000 **horsepower**. Andy Green, a British pilot, drove the Thrust SSC to a speed of 763 miles (1,228 km) per hour.

The fastest dragsters can reach speeds of 300 miles (483 km) per hour and cover a distance of one-fourth of a mile (400 m) in less than five seconds.

*Above, a dragster
Left, Andy Green and the record-setting Thrust SSC*

C A R
STOPPING

*A car's **parking brake** was originally called an emergency brake. It served as a second way to stop the car in the event that the regular brakes failed.*

C A R
DIRECTIONS

The U.S. assigns even numbers (I-70, for instance) to interstate highways that go east and west and odd numbers (I-55, for instance) to highways that go north and south.

Some cars today are equipped with computer screens that show driving routes

CARS IN THE FUTURE

Computers are responsible for the biggest differences between cars of today and those built 100 years ago. In today's cars, computers mix fuel and oxygen more precisely, tune engines as they run, and reduce exhaust gas pollution. Computers can receive signals from Global Positioning System (GPS) satellites to pinpoint the exact location of a car. Computer screens with built-in maps show drivers the best routes.

In the future, sensors may identify hazards on highways, and computers may automatically warn drivers of the dangers. Computers may even become auto-drivers that take over driving on long highway trips.

In 1953, U.S. President Dwight D. Eisenhower created the interstate highway system. Years earlier, he had crossed the U.S. by car. The trip took 62 days because of poor roads.

27

Above, a section of the vast U.S. interstate highway system

CAR
FUEL

Many gas stations in the U.S. sell gasoline that contains 10 percent ethanol, an alcohol made from grain such as corn. This helps to conserve gasoline.

Right, almost all cars today rely on gasoline Far right, an example of a hybrid car

The biggest concern about the future of cars is the use of gasoline as a fuel. The world's supply of gasoline will probably run out in a few decades, and scientists are looking for alternative sources of energy. Alcohol is a liquid made from wood or grain such as corn. Some countries in

South America depend on alcohol alone for car fuel and do not import gas from other countries. Electricity is another fuel option. However, electric cars are not very fast and can go only 100 miles (161 km) or so before the batteries need to be charged. Golf carts are the most common battery-powered electric vehicles.

Hybrid cars combine the best features of two engines. The most common hybrid has a small gasoline engine and an electric motor. When the driver is taking a short trip at low speed, the electric motor alone is used. At higher speed, or on longer drives, the gasoline engine takes over. In the year 2000, three different automobile makers put hybrid cars on sale in America.

29

CAR
COURSE

30

Several land speed records have been set on the long, straight course at Bonneville Speedway in Utah. The surface is salt left behind when a lake dried up 50,000 years ago.

Right, future cars may be sleeker and faster. Far right, a sign marking old Route 66

Hybrid cars and alternative fuels will one day make cars less polluting. But when they will come into wide-spread use is hard to foresee. In fact, it is difficult to predict what new features or shapes cars may have in the future. One thing is for certain, though. Cars will remain the world's most common mode of transportation for years to come.

C A R
ROUTE

Before Route 66 was replaced with interstate highways, people drove along this famous highway to reach California. Route 66 ran 2,400 miles (3,682 km) through eight states.

HISTORIC
OKLAHOMA
US
66
ROUTE

Glossary

A **catalytic converter** is a car part that reduces the pollutants in the vehicle's exhaust.

The **clutch** is a lever that briefly separates the drive shaft from the engine so a driver can shift gears.

Dragsters are specially built racing cars that travel at great speed over short distances.

The **drive shaft** is a rotating rod that carries power from a vehicle's engine to its wheels.

A car's **exhaust** is the fumes that come from the engine after fuel is burned with air.

An electric **generator** is a mechanical device that produces electricity when it is turned.

Horsepower is a measurement of the speed at which an engine does work. A 1.0 horsepower engine can lift 55 pounds (25 kg) to a height of 10 feet (3 m) in one second.

An **internal combustion engine** burns fuel inside the engine rather than in an external container.

A **parking brake** locks the wheels when a car is parked so it will not accidentally start rolling.

A **piston** is a disk that fits in a cylinder in an engine and moves by the force of exploding fuel.

Pollution is any waste material that makes air, land, or water less healthy for living things.

Sensors are electrical devices that measure changes in the operation of an automobile, such as air pressure or speed.

Spark plugs are parts that generate electric sparks to ignite the gas and air mixture in an engine.

A **steam engine** changes water into steam and uses the pressure of the steam to do work.

The **terrain** is the surface of the ground that a vehicle travels across.

Transmissions are sets of gears that change the amount of power that goes from a car's engine to its wheels.

Index